Wise at Heart

To our daughters, Robin, Traci and Jill, who make us laugh, cry and, hopefully, a little bit wiser. —RS and MS

To Solomon and Addy, my most unexpected and wise teachers, this book is from and for you.
Meggan, that desert kiss is ever blooming. Ann, my gratitude for your sure heart. — BH

A note on the photographs

The children pictured in this book are from all over the world. They represent 18 countries in all. We thank them for allowing us to take their photographs and share them with others.

Previous page: Vietnam. **Above left to right:** USA, Ethiopia, USA, Mexico, El Salvador. **Page 4: top** Turkey; **middle** Mozambique. **Bottom row left to right** USA, USA, USA, USA, Vietnam, Turkey. **Page 6:** Malawi. **Page 7:** USA. **Page 8:** Belize. **Page 9:** Ukraine. **Page 10:** New Zealand. **Page 11:** Malawi. **Pages 12/13: top** Vietnam; **bottom** USA. **Pages 14/15:** Vietnam. **Page 16:** USA. **Page 17:** Turkey. **Page 18:** United Kingdom. **Page 19:** USA. **Pages 20/21: top left and right** USA; **bottom left** Belize; **bottom right** Mozambique. **Page 22:** Turkey. **Page 23: left** Turkey; **right** Belize. **Pages 24/25: left to right** Vietnam, Canada, Mexico. **Page 26:** China. **Page 27:** Turkey. **Page 29: top** USA; **bottom left** Malawi; **bottom right** USA. **Page 30:** Vietnam. **Page 31:** USA. **Page 32:** Mozambique. **Page 33:** Ecuador. **Pages 34/35:** Ecuador. **Page 36: top** USA; **bottom** Turkey. **Page 37:** Belize. **Page 38:** Sudan. **Pages 40/41:** Malawi. **Page 42:** USA. **Page 43:** Malawi. **Pages 44/45:** Mozambique. **Page 47:** Liberia. **Pages 48/49:** USA. **Page 51:** USA. **Pages 52/53:** Turkey. **Pages 54/55: left** Belize; **right** Philippines. **Pages 56/57: top left** China; **top right** Mexico; **bottom** USA. **Pages 58/59: top** Belize; **bottom left and right** USA. **Pages 60/61:** USA. **Page 62:** USA. **Page 63:** USA. **Page 64:** Ecuador. **Page 66:** USA. **Page 67: top** USA; **bottom** China. **Page 69:** Mozambique. **Pages 70/71 left to right:** Turkey, Vietnam, Turkey, Mozambique.

Text and photographs © 2011 Milestones Project and Brody Hartman

Kids Can Press acknowledges the financial support of the Government of Ontario, through the Ontario Media Development Corporation's Ontario Book Initiative.

Published in Canada by
Kids Can Press Ltd.
25 Dockside Drive
Toronto, ON M5A 0B5

Published in the U.S. by
Kids Can Press Ltd.
2250 Military Road
Tonawanda, NY 14150

www.kidscanpress.com

Edited by Valerie Wyatt
Designed by Marie Bartholomew

This book is smyth sewn casebound.

Manufactured in Singapore, in 10/2010 by Tien Wah Press (Pte) Ltd

CM 11 0 9 8 7 6 5 4 3 2 1

Library and Archives Canada Cataloguing in Publication.

Wise at heart : children and adults share words of wisdom / by
    Broderick Hartman, Richard Steckel, Michele Steckel.

"A book of quotations by children and adults."

ISBN 978-1-55453-630-6

1. Wisdom—Quotations, maxims, etc. —Juvenile literature.
I. Hartman, Broderick II. Steckel, Richard III. Steckel, Michele

BJ1581.2.W585 2011   j170'.44   C2010-904766-4

Kids Can Press is a **corus**™ Entertainment company

Wise at Heart

Children and Adults Share Words of Wisdom

With
contributions by
Archbishop Desmond Tutu,
Jane Goodall, Tom Hanks,
Walter Cronkite, Eric Carle,
Frances Moore Lappé,
Greg Mortenson and
other elders and children
from around the world

By Brody Hartman, Dr. Richard Steckel and Michele Steckel

Kids Can Press

Wise Inside

Some wisdom to honor you from the inside out

"Everyone is a VSP — a very special person. You too are a VSP."

—Archbishop Desmond Tutu

You have no idea how good you are.

— John Graham

My heart wants to teach the world that EVERYONE has a great soul.

— Matthew, age 10

An older cousin of mine, a Quaker, taught me to listen to the still, small voice inside me. That voice some call the conscience, some call the good angel, some call God inside. Often it is hard to hear the voice, so I had to learn to be silent when listening (hard for a very talkative, antsy kid like me). I don't always hear that voice, but when I stop to listen, it always tells me to do the right thing, even when the right thing is difficult to do.

Believe in yourself. Touch the magic within — and pass it on.

— Jane Yolen

Young people tend to try on different personalities. Sometimes they borrow from friends or imitate pop stars — anything from a way of dressing to a way of speaking. But if you do this, what happens? You attract friends through a sort of false advertising. This means that your "friends" aren't tuned in to the real you. But if you are always yourself, you attract friends who love you the way you are — in other words, true friends. You'll be a lot happier this way, and you'll like yourself as well.

— Jerry Dunn

Trust what rises unbidden from your heart and then share it. The most beautiful gift you can give the world is who you really are, what you truly think, what you really love, what you believe.

— Juliana Forbes

All you need to be happy is to be surrounded by people you love and care about.

—Clark, age 15

Don't listen to people who don't believe in you.

—Maddie, age 9

Family is bigger than your parents and blood relatives. You can adopt and be adopted by anyone with whom you have a heart connection — which is easier to make than you might imagine.

— Marika Stone

Parents: Stop trying to be your child's friend — that's not going to happen. Be their ally. If you treat kids like adults, they will act more like adults. If you respect them, they will respect you.

— Sara, age 17

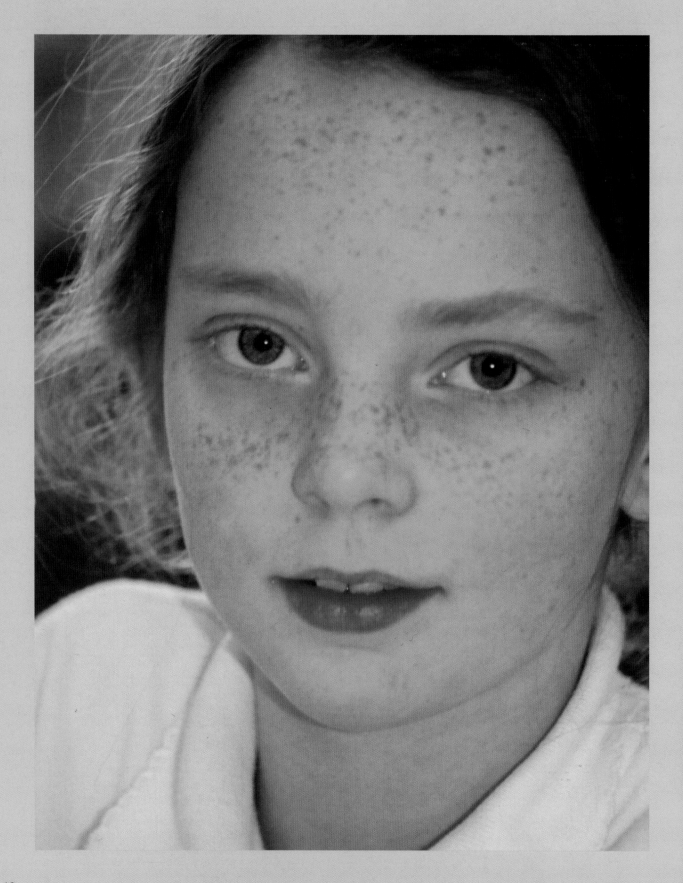

No matter what is happening in your life, how difficult things may be, you are bigger than the circumstances you are in. You amount to much more than the challenges you face. Challenges or problems you may be living through do not define who you are — YOU define who you are.

— Lee Sher

Dignity is priceless. You can't buy it.

— Yasmin, age 11

Stand up. Don't be scared.

— Emily, age 10

Have courage.

The courage to dream big dreams.

The courage to try new and difficult things when you know you may fail.

The courage to include those who are left out for whatever reason.

The courage to challenge injustice or cruelty, even though you may be the lone voice.

The courage to forgive others.

The courage to reach out to new friends at the risk of being rejected.

The courage to share your true feelings.

The courage to make yourself who you would like to be.

— Mary Gordon

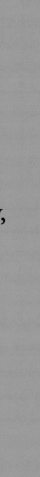

Think well of yourself, but don't say so.

— Tom Hanks

You are special. There is no one in the world just like you. Treasure yourself and take care of yourself, because you are truly unique and wonderful.

— Verla Kay

Believe in yourself.

— Nathan, age 11

Find what you love to do
(paint, write, sports), and if it
doesn't hurt anybody, keep doing it.
And doing it. And doing it.

— William Joyce

The greatest thing I could wish for any child is to care more passionately about something — books, music, frogs, pipe fittings, anything — than about the opinions of other people.

— Annie Barrows

Think about big questions — not to find easy answers, but to expand your mind. Why does the universe exist? What is the future of the human race? How do you live a good life? Be curious about everything.

— Jeanne DuPrau

Focus on experiences, not things.

— Sutton, age 9

The essence of the good life is connecting our passions with the biggest challenges of our time. If we care enough about something, we can learn what we need to know to make a difference. We don't have to wait for the "experts" to do it.

Life is a voyage of discovery. If we follow our curiosity and keep asking the next question and the next question about why we are here and where we want to go, our lives will be rich in love and satisfaction. Fear need not stop us, for it is just information and energy we can use to create the world we want.

— Frances Moore Lappé

I want everybody to know that even though I am only a child, I can do almost anything that I put my mind to.

— Marley, age 10

My wonderful mother told me, "Jane, if you really want something and you work hard and take advantage of opportunities and you never give up, you will find a way."

The most important message I have for anyone reading these words is that each one of us makes a difference every day. Our lives are meaningful and matter in the scheme of things. Young people, when informed and empowered, when they realize that what they do truly makes a difference, can indeed change the world.

— Jane Goodall

Peace Wise

What can we teach each other about the hard stuff, such as arguments, conflicts and even war?

"War solves nothing.
Peace solves everything."
—Myles, age 9

Hatred causes the greatest suffering in the world.

— *Marco, age 9*

Hate, if not the basest of human emotions, is very close to the bottom of the list. There is nothing redeeming about it. It is just short of being inexcusable.

Hate slams the door on civilized behavior. It denies us the possibility of finding paths to mutual understanding among all peoples and creeds.

It is not necessary to love thy neighbors. It is necessary only to understand them. Hate is the handmaiden of ignorance. It cannot long exist alongside knowledge and understanding.

— *Walter Cronkite*

The best way to honor someone
is to greet them with respect.

— Jacob, age 10

I think people in conflict should find a common
language to talk over their problems.

— Sasha, age 11

When I was upset by a school bully, our kindly school principal told me that we couldn't always choose what happened to us, but we could choose how we reacted to it. Problems were good teachers, he said. I wanted to know what bullying could teach me. He replied, "You will never do this to anyone because you know it hurts."

— Joy Cowley

People get angry at each other because they don't understand each other.

— Sedona, age 14

My mother used poetry and great literature to share wisdom. She had a favorite poem by Edwin Markham she would repeat when I was upset about social situations at school.

— Jolie Runyan Finkbiner

The Circle

by Edwin Markham

He drew a circle that shut me out —
Heretic, rebel, a thing to flout.
But love and I had the wit to win.
We drew a circle that took him in.

I believe that one of the most important skills a person
can develop is the ability to create relationships. This
doesn't just mean making friends. It also means taking
the time, and being willing, to get to know others who
are very different from you and finding out what your
commonalities are. Our commonalities are the
foundation for lasting understanding and dialog.

— Greg Mortenson

A hero is someone who opens up to something other than their own world. Someone who connects to people at their level and makes the world a better place. A hero is someone who doesn't care about themselves, who thinks of other people as family — he eats what they eat and he sleeps where they sleep.

— Amira Mortenson, age 13

Even the smallest act of kindness — lending a helping hand or comforting someone who is sad or upset — can create a powerful, positive difference in the lives of those you touch.

— Trudy Ludwig

To have a friend, you must be a friend.

— Kristine Hougard

When my friends fall, I help pick them up.

— Adam, age 5

We spend too much time focusing on physical traits, but we never look to the inside. Our pain comes from a lack of being accepted or prized. We must remember that we may not be privileged in the same way, but we are all gifted with existence.

— Baylin, age 11

We all have a responsibility to one another. Each one of us is human, and we all deserve respect, compassion and kindness.

— Marc and Craig Kielburger

Treat all people who are different with the most respect.

—Jessica, age 10

One piece of advice I received, which I believe came originally from Ralph Waldo Emerson, was "Always do what you are afraid to do." This does not mean being reckless, of course. It means to treat fear as a friend and source of information. Instead of steering away from fear, begin to walk, with alertness, in that direction, for it is often in that direction that your destiny lies. I have certainly found this paradoxical wisdom to be a valuable guide at many important choice points in my life. Courage!

— William Ury

It only takes one person to change the world.

—Jonathan, age 6

Help those people and places that are worthy and in need. As you struggle with these lifelong challenges, enjoy the beauties of the human family and the planet we call home.

—Joe MacInnis

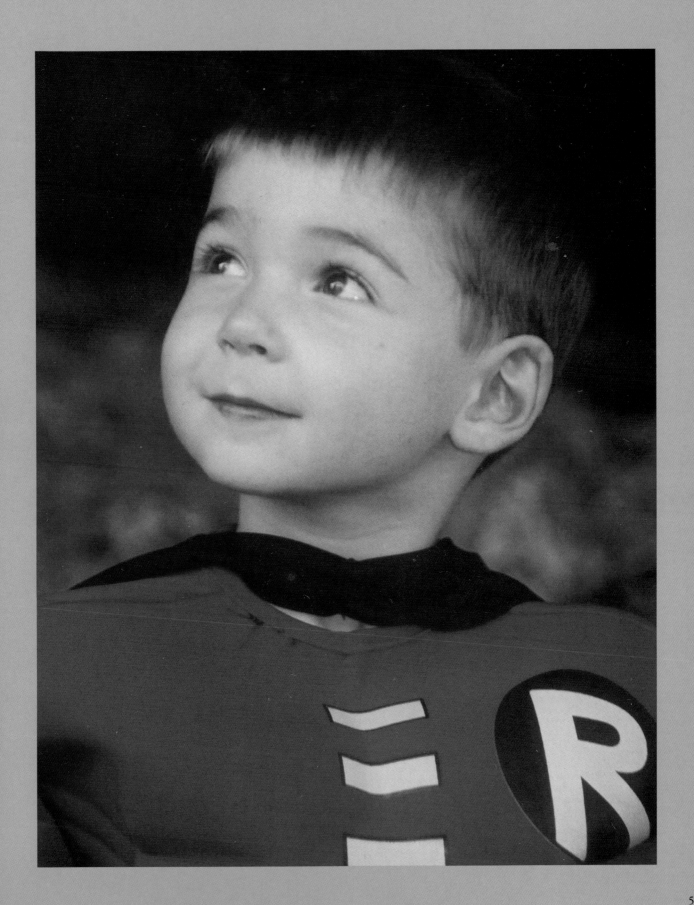

Nature Wise

Wisdom about and from nature

"Go play outside. Learn to love the land. It's hard to destroy what you love."

— *Lydia, age 16*

If trees could speak, they would teach us to be still, like them.

— *Michael, age 6*

Peace is the quietness of nature in us.

—*Jake, age 8*

I urge every child to find the quiet of nature, the rustle of the leaves on a tree, the trickle of the water in a river. The magic of nature is so important for children and for us all. And it is so important for us to have respect, reverence and care for our Earth and all of its beings.

— Martha Urioste

Notice stuff!

— Sandra Boynton

As a young boy, my father used to take me on walks in the woods, peel back the bark of a tree and show me the tiny insects that lived underneath.

I inherited from my father a love of nature and a fascination with all kinds of creatures. He showed me how to pay attention to the natural world, how to be kind and caring.

I would like to pass along this wisdom of my father's. Please, be kind. Enjoy the beauty of nature and the small wonders of every day. But most of all, be kind.

— Eric Carle

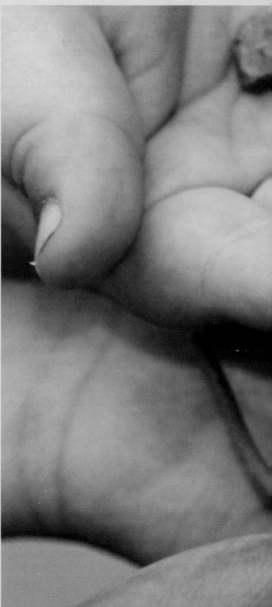

We and all the universe are all one and all essential parts of a jigsaw.

— *Tony Kirwan*

Consider nature as your family.

— *Aulia, age 16*

Nature teaches me to treat all things with respect. People, animals, trees, mountains — it is all the same, and we must never forget that.

— *Anna, age 15*

My parents always taught me that everything that you do in the world has an effect on someone or something else — even the smallest thing you do. So consider, before you do something, how it will affect the world.

— Brittany Bergquist

Everything in the world is from nature. So everything there *is* in the world is nature.

— Indigo, age 7

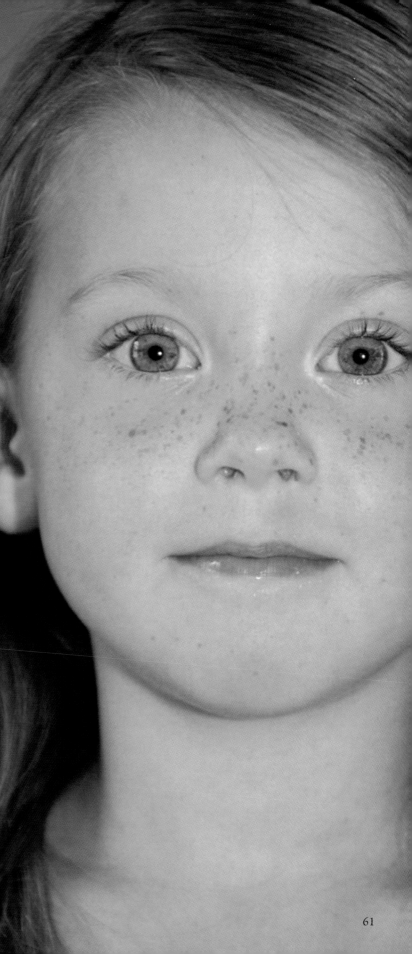

If a mountain could talk, it would mostly want to tell us that polluting is just killing ourselves.

— Gabe, age 13

Earth is our home — it's the only place we've got.

— Amanda, age 11, and Nick, age 8

Some Wise Good-byes

Some parting wisdom for your day, year, life, and miraculous journey of becoming the only YOU possible.

"Run, play, laugh, be kind, smile, try, rest, learn, explore, love, hug, help."

— *Michelle Quirk*

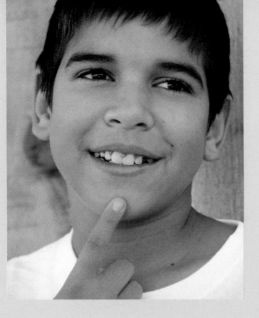

You can do anything once you put your mind to it, and you can always make a difference in the world.

— *Max, age 11*

Joy is a fire that is lit inside us when we do good things. The more right choices we make, the more brightly this fire burns, lighting up our path and showing us the way. The more wrong choices we make, the less brightly this fire burns, and the less we see the right path to take. In the dim light, we stumble and fall.

Joy comes from goodness, and goodness grows with joy. It guides us through times of little and times of plenty, times of conflict and times of peace. It changes our world. It makes it kinder. It outlasts everything. It outlasts us. So when we die, it lives on, lighting up the path of future generations — those who come after us — showing them the way even as they showed us the way.

— *Uzo Unobagha*

A Few Ways to Use *Wise at Heart*

In addition to turning the pages and landing wherever your heart or eyes take you, consider using *Wise at Heart* as a springboard for discussions, school assignments or even readings at family or community gatherings.

Our days are so busy that we rarely allow ourselves the time to absorb or reflect on new ideas. Try using *Wise at Heart* as a touchstone with your child or students by reading a page a day — discussing, reflecting and sharing. It's a wonderful way to begin or end the day.

Wisdom Catchers

How do we call forth our own wisdom as elders, caregivers, teachers and mentors? How do we listen for (catch) our children's wisdom? How do we create a society that celebrates wisdom as a means of bridging cultures, borders, ages, races and religions? How do we invite into our conversation those who falsely believe they have nothing wise to share?

Here are some "wisdom catching" ideas to explore and make your own. They involve one or all of the following: listening, discussing, documenting and sharing.

For Parents, Grandparents, Caregivers and Community Elders

1. Let your wisdom flow.

Write a letter to a child — your own, a grand child, a child in the community, or even more broadly, to the children of the world. In a "stream of consciousness," let your words flow freely. No judgment. No right or wrong answers. Just keep your hand moving. Write for fifteen minutes or even longer, if you wish. Use the prompts below as springboards or choose your own topic.

Dear_____:

• These things I know to be true about (nature, family, love, peace, my life, life's challenges, relationships, our family's cultural heritage, etc.) …

• This teaching or lesson has served me well …

• A bit of cherished wisdom I received as a child is …

• The most valuable wisdom I want to share with you is …

2. Catch your insights.

Review your writing with a highlighter in hand and circle (catch) anything that has energy, resonance or interest for you — this is where the gold is hidden. You can repeat step one to build upon your insights or simply create a list of what you discovered.

3. Share your wisdom with a child in whatever way you choose.

For Teachers

Using any of the themes touched upon in *Wise at Heart* (or others that are relevant to your community), feel free to explore some of these seed ideas:

• Ask your students to interview their grandparents or family elders.

• Have grandparents interview their grandkids for an eye-opening twist.

• Organize a trip to a local nursing home or adult community. Have your students interview and document (via video, photos, writing, etc.) the residents of the home. Create a "wisdom catching" assignment in which students comb through their content and find words or ideas that strike them as important. Distill the insights into a book of wisdom to offer the residents of the nursing home and other students.

• Ask students to identify and articulate the collective wisdom of your school. Create an exhibit or presentation of the findings.

• Identify a single piece of wisdom collected by your students and have them expand it into a larger project. Turn it into a play, a mural or a new series of interviews captured in a video.

• Have students identify the collective wisdom of their immediate community. Listen, discuss, document and share.

• Teach students how to distinguish between cultural chatter and wisdom.

• The word "philosophy" is from the Greek, meaning the love of wisdom. Mine the great minds of philosophers, such as Socrates, for new language about wisdom.

However insights are gathered, shared or discussed, it is our hope that wisdom is used to bridge the diversity of our voices, experiences and beliefs and to make wise decisions — great and small — in service to the common good of all beings.

With gratitude,
Brody, Richard and Michele

Adult Contributors

Annie Barrows is the author of many books for young people, including the Ivy and Bean series. She has also won wide acclaim for the adult novel *The Guernsey Literary and Potato Peel Pie Society*, which she completed when the original author, her aunt Mary Ann Shaffer, became ill.

Brittany Bergquist launched Cell Phones for Soldiers, Inc., at the age of thirteen. This nonprofit organization offers thousands of troops the opportunity to keep in closer contact with their loved ones. CPFS collects used cell phones, sells them to a cell-phone recycling company and uses the proceeds to send prepaid phone cards to soldiers.

Sandra Boynton is well known for her signature cartoon animal characters, especially those for children's books. She also creates characters for greeting cards and many other products, such as gift wrap, clothing, fabric, calendars, puppets and wallpaper. She has also written and produced songs for young audiences and text for choral music.

Eric Carle is the author or illustrator of more than seventy books for very young children. His best-known work, *The Very Hungry Caterpillar*, has eaten its way into the hearts of millions of children all over the world and has been translated into more than thirty languages.

Joy Cowley, a New Zealand writer, travels the world speaking to teachers, children, parents and other story lovers. She specializes in books for children who have difficulty learning to read. She has also written short stories and novels for adults.

Walter Cronkite was an eminent broadcast journalist often described as the most trusted journalist in the United States. He was best known as the anchor for the CBS Evening News, a post he held from 1962 to 1981. Among the many historic world events he covered was the death of President John F. Kennedy and the moon landings. He died in 2009.

Jerry Dunn is a writer of books and stories for magazines and newspapers. He has worked with National Geographic for twenty-five years as an editor, writer, columnist and guidebook writer. His travel writing has earned him three Lowell Thomas awards, the travel-writing equivalent of an Academy Award®.

Jeanne DuPrau writes books for young people and is particularly known for her novel *City of Ember*, a tale of human existence cut off from the natural world, which has become the centerpiece of a four-part series. She has also been a teacher, editor and technical writer.

Jolie Runyan Finkbiner is an advocate for children and teens through her work with community programs in Chicago. She is the director of the After School Community Enrichment and the Summer Success/ Summer Food Program as well as Crawford County Teen REACH of Robinson, Illinois.

Juliana Forbes is cofounder and creative director of Mothers Acting Up, an activist organization that inspires, educates and engages mothers to advocate for corporate and public policies that make children a priority.

Jane Goodall is an internationally renowned primate researcher who began studying chimpanzees in Tanzania in 1960. In 1977, Dr. Goodall established the Jane Goodall Institute (JGI), which continues her research and works to protect chimpanzees and their habitats. JGI is also involved in other community-centered conservation and development programs in Africa. Roots & Shoots, JGI's global environmental and humanitarian youth network, has almost 150 000 members in 110 countries.

Mary Gordon is an educator, child advocate, parenting expert and author. She is the founder and president of Roots of Empathy, an organization that provides classroom curricula to increase children's social and emotional competence and help them develop a stronger sense of empathy. Her 2005 book, *Roots of Empathy: Changing the World Child by Child*, has received high praise internationally.

John Graham is an author and speaker who teaches positive ways of handling challenge and conflict. Since 1983, he has been a leader of the Giraffe Heroes Project, an international organization that encourages people to stick their necks out for the common good.

Tom Hanks is a two-time Academy Award–winning actor well known for performances in movies such as *Philadelphia, Forrest Gump, Sleepless in Seattle* and *Saving Private Ryan*. He is also a director, executive producer and screenwriter. He is a strong proponent of environmentalism and, along with his wife, Rita Wilson, an advocate for a variety of organizations that support children and families in need.

Vincent Harding is an African-American historian and scholar of religion and society. He was active in the American civil rights movement in the 1960s and '70s and is best known for his work with, and writings about, Dr. Martin Luther King, Jr.

Kristine Hougard is a mother, a teacher and a case manager with Highline Academy in Denver, Colorado.

William Joyce is an author and illustrator of children's books, including *Buddy, Santa Calls, The Leaf Men and the Brave Good Bugs, A Day with Wilbur Robinson* and *George Shrinks*. Two of his books have been adapted as animated television series, and one was made into a live-action film. His illustrations have also appeared on many covers of *The New Yorker*.

Verla Kay began writing books for children while running a day care from her home. Since then, Verla has published short stories, historical picture books in rhyme and a biography, *Rough, Tough Charley*. She also teaches writing and illustrating children's literature.

Marc and Craig Kielburger are activists for children's rights through the organization Free the Children, which Craig founded in 1995 when he was twelve years old. Marc is the chief executive director of Free the Children, an international development and youth empowerment organization. Free the Children has built more than 500 schools in Asia, Africa and Latin America, providing education to some 50 000 children. It has also established more than 23 000 alternative income projects to help women and their families achieve sustainable incomes.

Tony Kirwan is an attorney and member of the Law Firm Network in Ireland and won a Pioneer Award in 2009 from the Global Equity Organization for outstanding contribution in support of GEO.

Trudy Ludwig writes children's books that explore the colorful and sometimes confusing world of children's social interactions. She is also involved in anti-bullying organizations. Her first book, *My Secret Bully*, grew from her daughter's own painful experiences.

Joe MacInnis is a physician-scientist, author and deep-sea explorer. He has led thirty expeditions into the Atlantic, Pacific and Arctic oceans and written ten books about undersea exploration. His work has earned him a number of honors, including his country's highest, the Order of Canada.

Frances Moore Lappé, an author and social change activist, is the co-founder, with Anna Lappé, of the Small Planet Institute, whose motto is "Living democracy, feeding hope." Among her sixteen books is the bestseller *Diet for a Small Planet.*

Greg Mortenson is the cofounder, with Dr. Jean Hoerni, and executive director of the nonprofit Central Asia Institute. Since 1993, he has dedicated his life to promoting community-based education and literacy programs, especially for girls, in remote mountain regions of Pakistan and Afghanistan. He is also the author of *Three Cups of Tea.*

Michelle Quirk is the author of *Back to Basics: An Old-Fashioned Recipe for Raising Happy and Healthy Children* and is the business development manager at First Foundation in Auckland, New Zealand. The foundation works to help academically talented and financially disadvantaged New Zealand students achieve their potential through higher education and have a positive impact on their communities.

Lee Sher is a pioneer in teaching sign language for babies, toddlers and young children. She is the author/producer, with Barbara Granoff, of a DVD entitled *Sign-A-Lot: The Big Surprise.* As an educator, she has learned that when hearing children learn sign language, they improve vocabulary, concepts, number recognition and reading and spelling skills, as well as their ability to express emotions.

Marika Stone is a cofounder of 2young2retire, an organization for people seeking rewarding experiences in a new career or life calling. She has been a teacher of English and writing, a journalist, a PR account executive and a small-business owner. She is also the author of *Too Young to Retire.*

Desmond Tutu, the eminent South African archbishop and activist, was for years a vocal opponent of apartheid. In 1975, he was appointed dean of St. Mary's Cathedral in Johannesburg, the first black man to hold that position. From 1976 to 1978, he was bishop of Lesotho and in 1978 became the first black general secretary of the South African Council of Churches. In 1984, he became the second South African to be awarded the Nobel Peace Prize. He is cofounder, with his wife, Leah, of the Desmond Tutu Peace Centre.

Uzo Unobagha is a writer and the author of *Off to the Sweet Shores of Africa and Other Talking Drum Rhymes,* a collection of more than seventy-five original nursery rhymes based on her Nigerian heritage. Her most recent book, *Grandma, How Do You Say I Love You?* is about the relationship between a girl and her Nigerian grandmother, who comes for a visit.

Martha Urioste, an elementary principal, implemented the first Montessori education program at Mitchell School in northeast Denver. She is the cofounder and former Family Star president of an Early Head Start site based on Montessori teaching. She has served the Denver public schools for decades and was among the first Latina counselors in that district, as well as its first secondary bilingual coordinator.

William Ury cofounded Harvard's Program on Negotiation and is currently a Senior Fellow of the Harvard Negotiation Project. He has served as an advisor and mediator in such diverse areas as corporate mergers, coal mine strikes and ethnic wars in the Middle East. He is the author of *The Power of a Positive No* and co-author, with Roger Fisher, of *Getting to Yes.*

Jane Yolen is the author of more than 280 children's books, including *Owl Moon, Devil's Arithmetic* and *How Do Dinosaurs Say Goodnight?* She is also a poet, a teacher of writing and literature and a reviewer of children's literature. Her books and stories have won many prestigious awards, including the Caldecott Medal.